The Dream Book

THE DREAM BOOK

DREAM SPELLS,

NIGHTTIME POTIONS

AND RITUALS,

AND OTHER MAGICAL

SLEEP FORMULAS

by

Gillian Kemp

Little, Brown and Company

Boston New York London

In memory of
my mother, Ruth, who visits my
dreams with premonitions.
To Rosie Posy,
my Yorkshire terrier, and her
godmother Katie Boyle.
To my father, Mike, and
my sister, Alison.
Also to Sharon and to John.
To my publisher Mary
and her associate Jennifer.
To my agent Chelsey.
To my artist Julia.
To you the reader. And also
to the one I love.

Contents

Hold a book, close your eyes,
open a page, and put your
finger on it. Open your eyes
and begin reading from
where you pointed.
The words are premonitory.

*D*reams are teachers, designed to make our desires come true. They allow us to discover our true destinies by disclosing nature's secrets through the language of the soul. They are our subconscious and the essence of our being. Dreaming is a form of clairvoyance, because it gives us inner vision that can attune us to our souls and to purer, higher forces, revealing the truth. The study and interpretation of dreams is known as *oneiromancy,* and dates back centuries. *Oneiro* is Greek for dreams, and *mancy* is Greek for divination. Ancient Greeks and Egyptians, and biblical figures such as Moses, Pharaoh, and Joseph in the Old Testament changed the course of history by believing that their dreams were prophecies from God. ¶ We all dream, even babies and animals. The sleep of dreams is light and easily recognized by rapid eye movement called REM. We do not dream during deep sleep, in which there is no REM. Light sleep and deep sleep alternate throughout the night. Our deepest sleep occurs in the first hour and a half. After that, the brain moves into light sleep and dreaming begins. We dream for about two hours a night, which adds up to several years over a lifetime. We do not sleepwalk during dreaming, because messages from the brain cause a natural limb paralysis. Just as a sleepwalker can "see" where he or she is walking with his or her eyes closed, so can a person whose spirit leaves the body during a dream "see" his or her body asleep with the body's eyes closed. What we "see" in a dream is the pictorial incarnation of creative thoughts. Your soul has superior, intuitive foresight and insight beyond the limitations of conscious thoughts and views. If you are lucky, you may even see visions at your bedside after waking. Such visions are called "dream traces" and disperse at your slightest movement. ¶ We are all able to receive prophecies, because dreams awaken us to our souls. Dreams that come true are proof of the soul's existence. The soul subconsciously receives supernatural pictures, words, and messages. Once your mind is focused on the phenomena of dreaming as a real experience, another, higher consciousness of the supernatural develops, because dreams are the language of the subconscious. ¶ Both past and future can be seen in dreams because dreams enable a person to make contact with his or her deepest aspirations and wishes, which are often subconsciously submerged. Dreams are wonderful problem solvers that tidy up and separate material differently than the conscious mind does. The subconscious mind presents dramatic symbols and exaggerated likenesses to attract our attention to problems. Dreams allow us to face problems while we sleep, so that when we wake up, we can solve conundrums the conscious, reasoning mind has failed to solve. The solution to a problem usually appears at the end of a dream, but sometimes a series of dreams brings the solution. Other dreams show the consequences of problems we may not consciously be aware of having. In some dreams, we imagine that a problem is solved, such as when we imagine we are awake but are actually still asleep because at that moment sleep is preferable. ¶

Dreams can speak in parables, analogies, and symbols already affiliated with the dreamer's mind, interpretation, and unique emotions. Different types of dreams serve different purposes. Dreams can be prophetic, giving a glimpse of what we can expect to happen in our immediate and more distant future. We can also "visit" living or dead loved ones in our dreams, and send and receive telepathic messages during sleep. Through dreams, we can discover the truths hidden by sleeping loved ones by speaking to them while they are asleep. All of this and more will be revealed in this magical dream book.

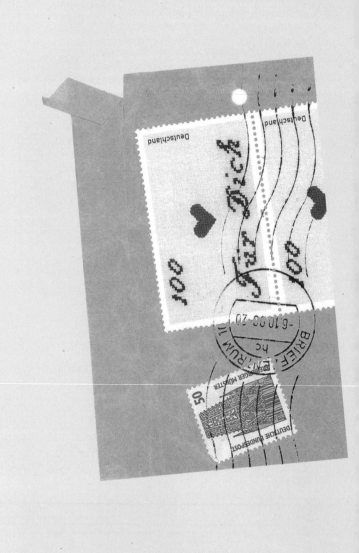

The five types of

Dreams

There are five different types of dreams: ordinary, lucid, telepathic, premonitory, and nightmare. They often blend and merge with one another.

ORDINARY DREAMS

During the day our conscious minds are active, but at night the subconscious takes over. Ordinary dreams are based on the activity of the unconscious in response to what we have seen or heard in our waking hours. Even a single thought can trigger a dream. Automatic unconscious stores of knowledge that have made an impression remain filed in the brain and unperceived until "read" by dream symbols, which are "the language of the soul." Events of the day and from years past are mirrored in the sleeping mind, as seemingly long-forgotten memories can resurface in dream imagery. The soul is particularly susceptible to the bygone memories that are brought to light through pictures in the mind's eye. In addition to being clairvoyant, dreams are also clairaudient, as we hear souls speak in our minds' ears. *Clairvoyance* means "clear sight." It is the supernatural ability to see people and events far away in time or location. *Clairaudience* means clear hearing. It is the faculty to hear with the mind's ear. Words spoken to us in our dreams should be taken literally, because such spiritual communication can show us how we should be when awake. You can get the best out of your future by understanding what a dream is saying to you pictorially and verbally.

LUCID DREAMS

A lucid dream is one that you can control because you are aware that you are dreaming. You can also decide what to dream about before going to sleep and then dream about the very thing that you planned to.

TELEPATHIC DREAMS

Telepathy, known as "the language of the angels," allows the dead and the living to speak in dreamland. In this meeting place, death is no barrier, and the living cross the threshold into a heavenly sphere of existence. This mental communication can also occur mind-to-mind between two living people. We may send our own or receive others' intentional or unintentional thoughts as mental visions in dreams. Extended telepathy during sleep is a communion between two worlds, the night-time world of the soul and the daytime world of the body.

[18]

PREMONITORY DREAMS

Premonitory dreams are similar to telepathic dreams in that your spirit leaves your body and ventures on a voyage of discovery. Premonitory dreams are special because they reveal the future and allow the dreamer to see truths that are not accessible in waking life. In telepathic dreams, we can also detect information about an imminent event. Dreams are the catalyst that put your body into motion to follow and fulfill your wishes and desires.

NIGHTMARES

Most nightmares are linked to early childhood, when we are inexperienced and therefore dependent on others. Before the age of three, we have not yet developed a sense of conscience and of right and wrong. Nightmares are representations of a suppressed, original fear commonly created by excessively strict parental or sibling moral standards and the threat of punishment in the face of innocence.¶ In nightmares you may perceive a warning for yourself or for a loved one. To be forewarned is to be forearmed: if you first see a frightful event in a dream, you can prevent harm from happening in waking life. For example, nightmares can warn against acting on impulse, as well as show that certain feelings and emotions are unhealthy.¶ Not all nightmares are nasty predictions or unwholesome signs. A nightmare may also relate to an old, unsolved problem that is so frightening to face that we are unable to continue to dream and the emotional terror wakes us in distress without offering a solution.

[19]

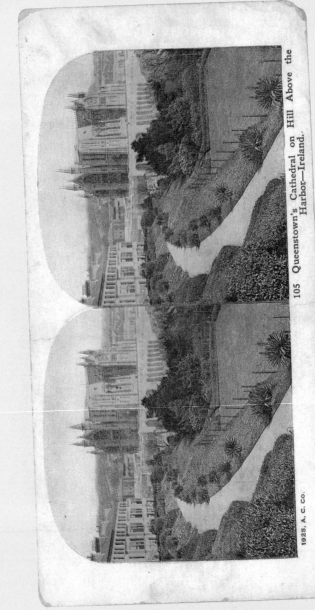

1925, A. C. Co.

105 Queenstown's Cathedral on Hill Above the
Harbor—Ireland.

RecUrring
dreams

It is said that your wish will
be granted if you count nine
stars in the sky and make a wish.
Count the same stars or
another set of nine stars on eight

Recurring dreams release repressed emotions and focus our attention on unsolved problems. Their aim is to restore our personalities back to complete, undamaged health. Some past experiences show where a problem originated but appear only in fragments. If we are scared to face a problem, we wake in fright or forget the dream that we just had. The same or a similar dream then recurs, presenting new versions and exaggerations until the message is understood and the cause of the problem is dealt with. Each time the dream is repeated, subconscious memory and imagination about the future merge further, improving our thoughts and actions until they finally suggest a solution. Even though each of us is unique, many people share the same recurring dreams.

BEING CHASED

This is a common dream in which the dreamer is often rooted to the spot, unable to move. The dream is a sign of anxiety and lack of confidence. It may relate to childhood, when you lacked the physical power to run away from a frightening experience, or to infancy, when you lacked the ability to walk. To be able to run when pursued in a dream reveals your wish to be wooed and also prophesies your successful achievement of personal ambitions and long-held desires.

more consecutive nights. After nine nights in total, your wish will begin to come true.

BEING NAKED
IN PUBLIC

Nudity uncovers a desire to express yourself and to be less self-conscious and secretive. If in your dream you find yourself inhibited and fearing public disapproval, this points to your frustration and difficulty in being yourself. Perhaps in childhood you were punished for seeking attention, causing you to grow up self-conscious and lacking confidence.

BEING UNPREPARED
FOR AN EXAM

[24]

To dream of being unprepared for an exam reveals a fear of failure in a current challenge. The subjects that you dream about may be questions on an exam in waking life.

CLIMBING

To see yourself climbing a ladder, a hill, or any other object shows an ambitious desire to make it to the top and is an omen that you are on your way to achieving your lofty enterprise. You may need to push yourself onward and upward to reach your desire. You will succeed if you reach the top in the dream.

It is said that to turn your

DINING WITH A PRESIDENT
OR CELEBRITY

To dream of dining with a VIP denotes a subconscious urge to gain admittance to a higher society. It can also be a premonition that you will be mixing in elevated social circles.

FALLING

Fear of failure is revealed by a dream of falling or being afraid of falling. You may be afraid of a moral decline or a lapse in ambition or business. You may be driving yourself too hard trying to reach a goal. It may also be [25] a premonition that precedes an avoidable setback or loss. Expect good fortune if you fall in a dream without being hurt.

FLYING

Flying represents a longing for freedom and a wish to escape constraints. It can also be a sign that you will transcend troubles and soar to great heights above and beyond the limits of your expectations, receiving praise along the way.

mattress on Sunday is a sign that you will lose your lover.

LOSING SOMETHING

Dreaming of losing something indicates insecurity about the lost object. It may be a premonition, in which case the loss can be avoided with your diligent care.

MEETINGS

When we dream of partaking in an activity with someone we know, that person is in the back of our minds, whether he or she is alive or dead.

[26]

MEETING THE DEAD

To dream of someone who has died means that you had a real meeting with that person, and his or her spirit is alive and well. This person has had a loving influence on you in life and will keep giving you help by meeting you in your dreams.

MEETING STRANGERS

We all encounter strangers in our dreams whom we neither know nor recognize. Whether the dreamer is male or female, an unknown woman or girl can represent our intuitions or a personification of the female personality. Men or boys in dreams, also irrespective of the gender of the dreamer, can reflect an inner masculine character. This is based on animus/anima (male/female), the principle that everyone has both a male and a female personality in his or her emotional makeup.

MISSING A PLANE OR TRAIN

A plane or train journey represents your personal journey through life. To miss either unveils a frustration at being unable to find your vocation or path in life, or to make as much progress as you would like. You may be too fearful to keep going forward. If in future dreams you catch the train, you will know that you are on the right track, have found your niche and achieved something.

[27]

OBJECTS COMING TO LIFE

A common object that comes to life in dreamland is a toy. This dream is a sign that you are maturing. You may be discovering new interests in subjects that you were once indifferent to, such as sports, music, religion, academics, art, or romance.

SWIMMING

Swimming reveals that your subconscious is encouraging you to attain your goal. The difficulty or ease with which you swim reflects how hard or simple your aim to achieve "the shore" will be. It may also relate to a birth trauma or the fear you experienced in learning how to swim.

Bad Dream
Superstitions

- "To dream of things out of season Is trouble without reason."

- To dream of a wedding, a white bird, or broken glass precedes someone's demise.

- It is bad luck to tell someone your dream before breakfast.

- To dream that a ring falls off your finger is an omen that you will lose a friend.

- To dream of losing a tooth is a sign that you will quarrel with a friend.

Keeping

a dream

Diary

*D*reams have an elusive quality and are spirited away into the ether as mysteriously as they come. The secret to remembering them lies in recalling dream components precisely at the moment when your dream begins to slip away, as you vaguely begin to move from the ethereal twilight world to the waking state. The best time to write a dream down is before even getting out of bed. For this purpose, buy yourself a hardback notebook that will become your personal prediction book. Don't allow yourself to wake up completely until you have cast your mind back and willed yourself to consciously and concisely remember your dream. Force yourself to recall objects, locations, conversations, and actions, as well as colors.¶ In your dream diary, write the date of your dream and whether you felt happy or disturbed about what you saw. Next, write or draw the sequence of your dream or dreams. If you remember only fragments, note those objects or remnants that you can remember. Since dreams are pictorial, you may find it easier to draw pictures as you saw them rather than interpreting your dreams into words. If conversations occurred, write those down too. Finally, under the heading "Prediction," hazard a guess as to how and when you think your dream will come true.¶ Once you begin to collect dreams, you will see that dreams do come true, whether they are inspired by beneficial spirits or by your own subconscious. Dreams are personal and related to your unique problems and experiences. You may see a pattern emerge where certain recurring personal emblems or verbal messages always precede good or misfortune that is then repeated in your waking life. This fixed symbolism will give you a common language for interpretation. ¶ At the very least you will see your dream as coincidental or as a previously rehearsed play. Some dreams may encourage you to follow an ambition by revealing the outcome, but may not necessarily show you what you have to go through or how long it will take to achieve. This can be good, as it prevents you from changing your mind about a course of action.

DREAM DIARY KEYS

When a dream comes true, tick it off in your book or draw a line underneath it and note the date. Write how your prediction matches what happens in your waking life. Perhaps stick matching colored stars or use corresponding numbers to link your premonition with your dream come true. You could use the first half of your diary for dream predictions and the second half for dream fulfillment. You could also have an "In-and Out-Tray" section for problems discovered and problems solved. Your dream magic book is unique to you. ¶ The strange imagery of dreams is reciprocal, made by your imagination from within and from without, like breathing. To dream freely, your psyche must be free rather than inhibited or limited by your desires or fears when making predictions. Only then can your sight have true clairvoyance. ¶ Your interpretation of the time for when an event might occur may be right in one way but wrong in another. Only when the event actually occurs in your waking life will you see how the timing of your dream was right but slightly different than what you expected.¶ As your dreams emerge and are recorded in your dream diary, your clairvoyance will naturally develop into a deeper, richer, more colorful and more audible experience. You will gain a stronger understanding of your own psyche and your personal rapport with higher forces that gently guard, guide, heal, and help you, revealing the way while you simply sleep.

33

Good Dream Superstitions

- "Friday's dream Saturday told Is bound to come true, however old."

- You will have "the luck of the devil" if you dream of the devil.

- To cry in a dream foretells coming joy and prosperity.

- To dream of a funeral is a sign of a wedding.

- To dream of a death is an omen of birth.

- To dream of music is a portent of a speedy marriage.

A~Z
dream dictionary

Зоологическ

The following dictionary is what dreams are made of. Enjoy unraveling your dreams to help you discover your destiny and reveal your soul's wishes.

Address:
Romance is forecast by a change of address. To see your present home address means that you will soon welcome a new love into your home. To write your address warns that you will see through insincere people who profess to be friends. An address connected to your career is an auspicious omen, promising a new success.

[37]

Advertisement:
To see or hear an advertisement is a prediction of imminent prosperity in work and fulfillment of ambition. You will find what you seek and get what you want, whether it is a job, club membership, or second-hand bargain.

Airplane:
Flying means that you are eager for a speedy change of circumstance and that you will soon rise to new heights. If you are in a plane that never takes off, a heartfelt wish will be granted after a delay. To miss a flight reveals a fear of missing an attainment that you may still achieve quite capably. If you see a bird's-eye view from a plane, you will be a highflier. A plane

It is believed to be lucky if you empty the contents of your pockets once you have landed.

crash seen in a dream may be one that you soon hear or
read about in the news.

Altar: An altar predicts a marriage made in heaven,
perhaps with your current lover. If you are single, you
are about to meet someone new but will have to stand
on ceremony at first and slowly dispose of formalities
for the relationship to develop correctly. Keeping
him wanting and waiting will draw him closer than if
you tell him your desires. Great joy is coming to you.
A church aisle also foretells a marriage and the meeting
of your life partner.

Anchor: The appearance of an anchor in a dream is
[38] an omen to have faith in your hopes and of wishes being
fulfilled. You will be delivered from existing problems.
It advocates holding on to family ties and ambitions in
which you have invested time and constant effort. To
see an anchor being dragged is a sign that your foundations are slipping.

Angel: One of the most favorable dreams of all, to
dream of an angel promises you enjoyment and high
honor. Protective invisible forces from another world
will bring good fortune and peace. Lovers will cele-
brate love, an engagement, or marriage, and possibly
all three.

Animals: Friendly, healthy, docile animals are good
signs of forthcoming creature comforts. To dream of

A cat sneezing on your wedding
day is said to be a sign
of a happy marriage.

finding an animal shows that you will get a new pet. To lose an animal shows that you may lose an ailing creature. When you dream of a specific animal, it has special meaning.

Bear: You may suffer cruelty at the hands of a crude man or woman.

Bull: Your father or a fatherly figure will influence you.

Cat/Kitten: You will be lucky in youthful love.

Dog/Puppy: You will put your faith in those who guard and guide you.

Elephant: You are becoming wiser and stronger. Clouds of doubt are disappearing.

Guinea Pig: Your comforts are close to home, a tie not to be forgotten.

Horse: With the speed of a horse, you will race through space and time; no hurdles are insurmountable.

Leopard: Someone you know may change superficially but not within.

Lion: Good will win over evil. Strength is on your side. You may be a born leader.

Mice/Rodents: A warning not to stay up all night and sleep all day.

Monkey: Fun is in store.

Pig: Someone you think of as impure has pure intentions.

[39]

Having an unknown dog following you is believed to be a sign of luck.

Rabbit: You are in for a lucky spell and may meet a valuable friend.

Sheep/Lamb: Purity and innocence will best determine your actions.

Squirrel: You will be accumulating small gains to achieve something worthwhile.

Tiger: Expect good news in the autumn, a time when animals change their coats.

Turtle: You may develop spiritually by nourishing yourself on ancient wisdom. You may discover many lifetimes of experience within yourself to draw on when faced with difficulties.

Wolf: Danger threatens around each full moon and especially around the next one.

[40]

Atlas:
Travel is forecast by a dream of an atlas. You may go to a far-off location or to a district that will have an important, pleasing impact on your life. New pathways will appear for you to develop through the impending visit.

Automobile:
Expect a speedy change if the automobile in your dream is speeding. An out-of-control vehicle mirrors your feeling of lacking control. A comfortable ride is a sign that you are on course. If you are taking a driving test in your dream, you will pass in waking life. If you are being driven and you dislike the ride, the driver may be someone attempting to override your interests.

If you push someone else's baby in a carriage, you will soon

Award: You will pass a sport, medical, or academic test, win the lover of your dreams, or achieve recognition and even fame in your chosen enterprise. With positive effort, you could win it all.

Baby: A bright new opportunity to nurture and cultivate a project beckons. Holding a baby means that you will encounter a pleasing situation. A crying baby precedes a disappointment and may show that inwardly you are desperate for help. A crawling or walking baby reveals that you are taking steps toward independence but that you would be unwise to assume that you are safe without superior guidance. A child symbolizes that you will experience a great spiritual change. This dream can also represent you as a youngster.

[41]

Backpack: You will be embarking on a new venture, globe-trotting, perhaps to an exotic location. You may also be moving away from difficulties or illness.

Ball: A ball game signifies good news and the removal of obstacles.

Balloon: Whether it is a hot-air or helium balloon, you will ascend worries and experience fleeting moments of lighthearted happiness and freedom on the way to achieving your long-term high ideals. Delays are des-

be expecting your own.

ignated by a descending balloon or by foggy, misty, or cloudy air around the balloon.

Band: If you enjoyed the music, you will hear pleasing news. If the music was not to your taste, you will hear unpleasant news or gossip involving you. If you aspire to become a musician, a big band playing is a sign that you could one day be part of a successful band.

Bandage: If you dream of a bandage, a wound will heal soon. Your soul realizes that past mishaps and wounds need not mar your future.

Bank: You will receive a boost in confidence from people who trust and value your opinions. You are urged to direct your talents positively rather than to keep them locked away. A financial windfall may appear, most likely through hard work.

Barefoot: You have an urge to be free and are warned against foolishness that may damage your reputation. The people you saw when you were barefoot are potentially harmful to you.

Bath: A change is about to occur in your life. A hot bath foretells luxurious surroundings and an inner wish for comfort from your mother. An unpleasant bathroom shows failure before happiness.

It is believed to be unlucky to get out of bed backward.

It is said to be a sign

Beach: A sunny beach reveals inner contentment and a move toward loving, emotional happiness. Problems precede contentment if the beach is stony. To be working on a beach means that your chosen career will be one of certain freedom and happiness, and involve travel. To notice or pick up a shell is a surprise of love and a windfall of money earned by loving what you do. With the tide of time beckoning, you will find undiscovered shores.

Bed: Making a bed means that someone you have met has bed in mind. If you are single be prepared, for someone new is about to appear. A pillow shows a kind person will help to ease your worries. An unfamiliar bed shows that you will stay away from home.

Beepers/Pagers: A dream of a beeper or pager is a sign that someone you know is searching his or her soul for you. The person may not show it, but he or she is feeling that he or she has done you an injustice.

Bells: Bells are a sign of happy changes in love and progress. Expect a marriage proposal if you are single and news of a birth for a couple. If the bells are alarms, be warned of treacherous deceit in love, friendship, or business.

Bicycle: You are being set in motion to move on or break bonds with someone or with a familiar situation.

of luck to sneeze while making the bed.

Doing so will be easy or difficult according to the ease or difficulty of the bike ride.

Birds: A good omen, birds signify your soul. A bright new day is dawning. As winter draws to a close, birds start singing a happier tune. Your life will cheerfully flow into spring on a happy note of freedom. Low-flying birds show that current earthbound problems temporarily restrict you. High-flying birds reveal a spiritual desire for freedom. You will attain your heaven-blessed wish. Birds of prey are a warning to be cautious about where you place your trust. Singing birds denote happy news. A dead bird means news of a death. An egg is the portent of a birth or a new mystery in your life. A nest indicates an approaching comfortable life-style. A feather means that you will be an example to others.

> *Blackbird:* Happy news is winging its way to you.
> *Canary:* Happiness with a lover will be limited by necessary duties.
> *Cuckoo:* You or a loved one may be unfaithful.
> *Dove/Pigeon:* You will have happiness in love. A new lover will arrive if a dove flies toward you. You will part company if the dove flies away.
> *Duck:* You will overcome an insecure situation and carry out your intentions.

To bring a bird's egg indoors invites trouble into the home.

Eagle: Your higher self will destroy baser forces. You have prophetic powers.

Owl: A sign to remain wise or be wiser.

Parrot: A warning to reconsider your actions to avoid idle gossip. You may unthinkingly reveal a secret.

Peacock: A reminder that beauty is skin deep and your soul immortal. Wealth is coming from a family member.

Robin: Someone is possessive of you.

Seagull: Expect news from a distance and the return of a traveler.

Stork: A sign that you will journey far.

Swan: You or someone else may be struggling beneath a serene appearance. Expect financial prosperity.

[45]

Birthday: Your birthday is going to amaze you with good news and a happy surprise. You will be congratulated and one wish will certainly come true around the time of your birthday. Good luck will befall you if you see a birthday card. Your wishes will come true if you see a birthday cake. Every birthday and forever after, divine intervention will bring you a special gift the week or two around its date. Birthdays may always link you to warm people.

Blanket: Comforting reassurance will protect you. However, schemers may want to smother and restrict you if you disliked the blanket. Be careful whom you cuddle and trust.

Blood: To bleed means sacrifice. Common sense may tell you to reconsider and perhaps end a situation your heart would like to continue. Bloodstained clothes reveal that you feel a stain on your character or are about to by going against what you know is right.

Boat: The right assistance will arrive to help you sail through troubled emotions or physical problems. You may enjoy a more carefree time on vacation by the sea.

Body: Success is at hand if you were happy with your body in your dream. Weight loss means that other people are sapping your strength; weight gain means that you are a strain on others. If you are trying to lose weight, the slimming will now begin and you will succeed with surprising ease. Sometimes a particular part of your body is the focus of a dream.

> *Arms:* You are going to be undertaking a new activity but should guard against the unforeseen.
>
> *Ears:* Expect to hear good news if you are happy with your ears and bad news if your ears bother you. Your right ear represents words of malicious gossip, your left means that someone in love with you cannot stop talking about you to his or her friends.

An itching right eye is said to be an omen of coming laughter and an itching left eye a sign of tears.

Eyes: You will meet a new lover or begin a new venture. You may need to look beyond the appearance or deeper than the surface, because something may not be as it appears at first sight.

Feet: You will find the necessary support to take you forward, although you may be in a vulnerable position and open to attack if your heel predominated in the dream. Aching feet precede a quarrel.

Hands: A heavenly hand leads you through life. If your right hand was featured more than the left, your rational, logical sense should currently guide your actions to protect you from harm and give you strength. If your left hand predominated, it is a sign to follow your heart.

Head: A reminder to question whether your actions are at one with yourself and the world, especially with those who mean the most to you.

Mouth: Speaking to others expresses your psychic energy and inner personality. What you put into your mouth is external. Inner states and outer forces meet at your lips. If the inside of your mouth is featured, you have the power to change something that does not feel right to your higher self. If the outside of your mouth predominates, your impulses need steadying to avoid self-harm.

If you knock one of your elbows gently, knock the other one for good luck.

Book: A new chapter will begin a crystal-clear story that you will write in your personal book of life. This dream is also a warning to learn from experience and to avoid making the same mistakes you see people around you making. A pile of books represents a time of solitude or study and comfort.

Bottle: Your feelings may be bottled up and ready to explode. A full bottle means forthcoming frivolity and an increase from an unexpected source. An empty bottle shows that your deepest needs remain unfulfilled and that you are likely to experience reverses and loss. Spilled bottles show domestic troubles. Broken bottles divulge that a spiteful, jealous person may inflict harm on you.

Box: You have a subconscious desire to express your femininity. In your career, an opportunity will come along that has more potential than you initially realized.

Bride: A wedding reveals that your soul is married to your spirit, a personal guardian angel that guides your soul. If you are the bride in the dream, you will soon marry. If you see your own wedding cake, you are about to be pleasantly surprised. To see someone else as a bride is a sign that your partner's affections might be torn between two sweethearts. To be kissed by a bride is a sign that you may inherit money. Confetti is an omen of social success. A wedding procession or gathering means that you are going on a lucky journey. To see a bridegroom in a dream means that delays will thwart your romantic hopes and wishes. If you are a bridesmaid, someone wants to seduce you without a commitment.

Bridge: The change you desire is about to occur through your consistent and willing effort. You are tuned into someone else's present and future thoughts, and are making a transition to a new path. Your strong spirit helps you to rise to bright new horizons.

Broken Bone: Your safety is threatened. A short, minor illness or emotional upset may occur through your own or another's actions.

[49]

Broom: You will make a clean sweep by moving away from a negative situation and embarking on a new venture of sincere growth and prosperity.

Cage: To cage an animal precedes a loss. If you nearly caged the animal you will regain something or a situation that you thought was lost to you. To be caged represents a feeling of entrapment.

Camera: A camera reveals that you will be looking at a situation from a new angle and seeing a different picture. Others may see another you in a changed environment.

Camp: A military camp shows that your self-discipline will pay off. A vacation camp reveals relief and a fun time to look forward to with inspirational company.

Candle: A new, dazzling opportunity will imbue your life. A candelabra promises that your destiny is about to be enhanced by enduring, bright, and creative activity in unusual places. One lit candle may represent a birth in the family. Unlit candles precede disillusionment. An extinguished candle is an omen of the news of a death.

[50]

Carpet: You will meet new acquaintances on new ground. The more colorful the carpet, the richer the experience will be. Red carpet means that you can expect especially good treatment. Soiled, frayed, or threadbare carpet warns that the company you keep could damage your health and finances.

Castle: A castle can represent your higher self, your body being the mansion of your soul. You can achieve an unattained ambition, because the proverbial castle in the air is now within your grasp. The unexpected will materialize, and so too may your knight in shining armor.

It is believed that sitting next to an empty chair tempts bad luck.

There will be an

CD: A claustrophobic phase may arise where you overly depend on reason to surmount difficulties that cramp your style. If you trust your intuition, difficult problems will be solved with less conscious effort.

Cell Phone: You will be traveling, but bonds and lines of communication will not be severed. You may receive a message from people in high places.

Chair: An empty chair signifies a reunion, while a comfortable chair indicates a rise in status. An uncomfortable seat shows discomfort ahead. A rocking chair means loved ones will intervene and help in a current or future dilemma. Stacked chairs represent moving to a new house.

[51]

Chocolate: You will taste sweet success in life.

Christmas: If Christmas is out of season, this dream is especially lucky. An important event is about to occur for you close to your home. It may precede a lucky twelve months bringing all the joys of Christmas. A fairy on top of a Christmas tree reveals that someone holds you in high esteem. It predicts that you will be adored and loved. Your light shines far is the message revealed by lights, ornaments, and tinsel on a Christmas tree. A nativity scene relates to family unity being strengthened. It can also represent that you delight in your dream of a baby lying in a crib. It predicts a

emergency in the home if a chair falls over.

healthy baby who will have far to go. Presents represent a puzzle as to what is in them. You will happily solve the riddle of a problem difficult to answer, just as you will when you open presents on Christmas Day. Santa's red suit shows how you want to display to others a paternal man you are thinking of and love. An opportunity will arise.

Church: A prayer will be answered. Peace will prevail over current emotional turmoil if a church or temple is featured. Being inside the building reveals luck in love. A baptism reveals a wish fulfillment. You have made a spiritual connection where the light in your soul will never be extinguished.

[52]

Cigarette: Smoking is a sign of trouble ahead. You may suffer a bad loss in a financial transaction. To accept a cigarette foreshadows making a wrong move.

City: Advantageous documents will arrive. To be lost in a city means that you feel alienated and need a trusted, experienced person to direct you.

Clock: An encouraging sign to follow your own feelings and to waste no more time vacillating. If you notice the time on the clock's face, something important will happen to you at that hour of the day. A wristwatch is more personal than a clock. Its tick is like a heartbeat and it is usually worn on the left wrist, so the occurring event will be close to your heart. A new lover will

It is said to be unlucky to speak while a clock chimes

appear or an estranged lover will reappear, and your love affair will run like clockwork. A moment when someone asks the time of day may be significant. If you leave somewhere early, an event will happen soon. If you leave late, the event will happen later than anticipated.

Clothes:
Changing or buying clothes in a dream represents that you are changing your personality. Uncomfortable or unattractive clothes reveal dissatisfaction with yourself or a situation.

Clouds:
You will receive a pleasing message, bringing a welcome breakthrough in your affairs. Something good will clear the air and shine through. The situation will be resolved quickly if the clouds are light colored. Dispersing clouds reveal a change in your mood.

Coffee:
Coffee with milk predicts a meeting with a fair-haired stranger, while black coffee predicts a dark-haired stranger. Love will be blighted if coffee is spilled.

Colors:
At times a specific color may prevail in a dream. Bright colors represent optimism.

Black: You may have future cause to feel shame and sorrow, but it is not inescapable fate. You have the freedom of choice.

Blue: Your health is good, your thinking is clear, and your immediate future will be carefree if you are true to yourself and fair to others. There is hope.

Brown: You may need to return to your roots or the roots of an event to branch out, blossom, and flower.

Gold: By perseverance you will be reveling in the glory of achievement.

Gray: Depression may hold you back from realizing your true worth.

Green: Your natural versatility makes you kind and forgiving.

Orange: Cruelty, pride, ambition, and selfishness may emerge in you or someone you know.

Pink: Romance and love are coming to woo you.

Purple: Nostalgic memories may make you reminisce on what might have been. Thoughts of someone in the past may inspire you to begin or continue an enterprise.

Red: Supernatural forces are leading you to happy, passionate, and sensual love.

Silver: A change to good fortune will make past tension disappear, bringing emotional happiness. Additional pleasure will arrive with small monetary gains.

Turquoise: Trust your fate and have faith in your destiny. A marriage is forecast, as is a change of heart and reconciliation if the turquoise changes to another color.

White: Pure in thought, you will be forgiving people their past mistakes without humiliating them. Your own path ahead is bright and clear. You will shine provided you do not allow others to sidetrack you from your beliefs or goals. You can achieve this if those who are likely to knock you off course orbit around you, instead of you adjusting to them.

Yellow: In your own life and in the lives of those you meet, your keen intuition sheds an optimistic light in darkness.

Computer: Everything that you see, hear, and do from the moment you are born is registered in your brain, which is like a computer. You will be taking great strides in your studies and career and perhaps embarking on a new academic and educational course.

Computer Malfunction/Crash: A malfunctioning or crashing computer relates to a fear of matters not running smoothly. It may precede a hitch or mishap in current affairs your mind is focused on.

Concert: You may be reviving a talent or a relationship if the music is pleasing. News will take you to palatial places or beautiful countryside. However, if you found the music jarring or inaudible, you will be confronted with an embarrassment.

Cooking: By proportioning the right ingredients at the appropriate moment, you will have all the magical ingredients to love and be loved, and to look after

It is said that food stirred in a counterclockwise direction is a sign that someone from your past will reappear.

yourself and others. If you enjoy cooking, all is well. If you are flustered or resent it, your love is misplaced. Cooking outdoors means you may wrongly devote care and attention to people who should be entertaining and nourishing your needs.

Credit Card: Someone may be giving you a false sense of security. You may soon discover that a person you believe to be reliable lacks genuine commitment.

Cross: You may struggle with the agony a quarrel causes and might need faith in the face of adversity before the other person approaches you for reconciliation.

Crowd: A family get-together may occur. To be part of a crowd is a sign of your popularity. If the crowd parts and you are left alone, you will stand out from the crowd and rise above the norm in a current or future endeavor. If you feel uncomfortable in the crowd, this is a warning to guard against theft and potential danger in busy places. If you are left out of the crowd, a friend will gain you admittance into a closed circle of friends or colleagues.

Crown: A regal crown shows that your life will be one of extraordinary wealth. A floral crown means that your own efforts will be crowned with high achievements and a perfect love match.

A child who cries long

Crying: Your own tears foreshadow sad news. If you see someone else cry, a loved one needs your sympathy and understanding.

Cup: Your whole personality including your heart and soul are symbolized. If you feel happy with the cup, happiness will be yours and you are at peace with yourself so far. Events around the cup may reveal where your happiness lies. A cracked cup means you may feel your spirit has been broken by disappointment, and it may be an omen that existing happiness is about to be marred.

~*D*~

Dance: Energetic dancing reveals that you will be filling your time and space creatively. Dancing with arms linked to form a chain means you will have an intimate relationship. If dancing made you feel unhappy, you lack enthusiasm.

Dating: If you enjoyed the dating in your dream, you may soon meet someone you like or dislike at first sight and not know why. It may be the person's walk, smile, or eyes that attract your subconscious observation. Your intuitive judgment more than your conscious thoughts will lead you to determine the outcome of the relationship.

is said to live long.

Death: For some, this is a dream of opposites. You may hear news of an engagement, wedding, or birth. If you are ill, it is a sign that your health is being restored. A corpse signifies the end of a love affair or phase in life. You may part ways with a friend if a coffin is involved. A burial means that you feel overwhelmed by pressure or problems. A hearse shows release from tension, and a skeleton inheritance. A grave is a sign of heartache. To dream of a relative dying may relate to a part of you dying that is represented by the person. For example, if a younger sibling dies, you may be losing your immaturity.

Dentist: Unless a dental appointment is on your mind, to lose teeth is a sign of an ongoing quarrel with a friend or a family feud that you need to end, because you need to grow up, and baby teeth fall out in early childhood. To have braces fitted to your teeth means that a special project can succeed if you begin it cautiously and with the right tools and support. Brushing or cleaning teeth reveals that you are about to be kissed.

Desert: A desolate phase in life may bring feelings of loss and loneliness, but the isolation will work to your advantage by enhancing the spiritual side of your nature. A bright thought beyond your normal comprehension may illuminate a new way ahead for you, like the sun shining on a barren desert.

It is said a wedding
and a birth always follow

Devil: This is sometimes a dream of opposites and luck. The devil is a master of disguise; a character of lust, not love; often silvery tongued; and good-looking and not easily recognizable. A married man or woman or someone from the wrong walk of life may bring a morally disagreeable situation to you.

Diamond: Expect sparkling engagements. In Sanskrit the word for diamond is *dyu*, meaning "luminous being." A sparkling romantic or career engagement will appear that will enable you to shine. You possess moral treasures and intellectual riches. A lover may propose.

Doctor: Visiting a doctor means that you wish to be taken care of. You may be telling yourself to respect your health by eating more natural and fewer processed foods. Taking pills and medicine or having an injection means that something external is being absorbed internally. If you react adversely, it is a warning that someone or something close is bad for you.

Door: A door divides. A closed door means that you are protected against someone or something that you do not want. If the door is open, you may gain access to someone or something that you want and new doors may open for you.

Drowning: This fear dream shows that you feel submerged by overwhelming problems and out of your depth. Being stubborn may bring you a difficult time

a death. The three are inextricably linked.

ahead, but if you survive the waters, you will survive your problems. To dream of someone else drowning means joy will follow sorrow.

Earthquake: You may be running a risk that could disrupt the foundations of your existence. This could be a sign of an untimely pregnancy for you or for someone else.

Eating: A good meal predicts a contented love life, while being hungry reveals that you desire more love. If you dislike the food, are eating something you normally would not, or if the food is spoiled, you may question whether you are damaging those nearest and dearest to you by focusing your attention on less-worthwhile people. If you find the food hard to swallow, what or whom you want is going to be difficult to get.

Elevator: An ascending elevator means progress. A descending elevator means regression. To be stuck in an elevator shows that you feel that you are not making the necessary progress to get you where you want to be.

E-mail: A friend may be trying to tell you something but cannot find the words or courage. You may be reestablishing contact with someone you have not seen or spoken to for some time. If you have fallen out with someone or lost contact, perhaps you should make the first move.

Engagement: To become engaged reveals the fruition of your plans and may foretell a new career or romantic engagement.

Envelope: Startling news you send or receive will be good or bad according to the appearance of the envelope. If the ink is smudged or if the writing is unusually divided, don't delay a matter that requires your attention. A torn envelope means you will quarrel with a friend or that news you are expecting may dash your hopes. A pretty envelope is a sign that you will soon receive happy news, such as a social engagement or a new job.

[61]

Face: Important events are about to begin. Smiling faces mean that people you are about to meet will make you happy socially or in your career. Seeing an unknown face reveals that your restlessness will be gratified by a journey or visit you are longing to make.

Fairies: You are gifted with extraordinary powers, visible even when you perform everyday chores. A magical, dramatic occurrence will change your lifestyle because fairies personify your soul.

Family: A family represents an embryo of the world at large. A large family gathering shows prosperity ahead, and you will be invited into a new family circle. Family sadness in a dream precedes bad news for relatives.

> *Father:* A dream of a father represents your conscious morals rather than your instincts. A father in happy and loving circumstances shows that you agree with the restrictions of wise advice and codes for correct conduct. Difficulty in your dream with your own father or with someone else's father shows rebellion against your own conscience and inner control, even though you may love your father devotedly.
>
> *Mother:* Femininity deeply and strongly rooted in your soul wisely guides your intuition. You are being nurtured and cared for, and nurturing is a quality you will also develop. Your mother will be there for you when you need her at any time in your life. Romance in the air carries signs of heavenly approval. You may feel a need to return to the place where you were born.
>
> *Sister:* What happens to your sister may represent what is about to happen to you, as she may be part of your psyche.
>
> *Brother:* Your brother or someone else's brother may represent another side to your personality. Events may relate to a future adventure. You may

[62]

meet or know a woman who would like to have a relationship with your brother. Your knowledge may be just what she needs for comfort.

Grandparents: You feel a strong sense of duty to your moral conscience.

Fax: Expect speedy news relating to your career or finances. You will quickly get a good result by dealing with business and vocational concerns.

Fields: You may feel someone or a situation is crushing your individuality, but you will soon free yourself from the oppression, because fields represent freedom. A plowed field means that you should put your plans into action and wait for the harvest. A green field or field full of crops means you will soon reap rewards for seeds sown.

[63]

Fight: You have obstacles to overcome before receiving a little success with current plans. You may suffer jealousy, disapproval, or spite from friends. To see others fighting is a warning to be cautious with money and financial commitments.

Fire: Your spiritual energy and physical passion are both about to be ignited. A cozy, comforting fire is reassurance of eternal light in your life. A plan you have been working on may now receive the spark it has needed. To stoke a fire reveals that you arouse someone's ardor. A fire out of control shows you may be playing with fire and are likely to get your fingers burned by self-destructive behavior. To escape from a fire means you will escape from an existing danger. To see a firefighter shows you desire a masculine man to sweep you off your feet.

Fireworks: Expect great animation in your love life; thrilling but risky moments lie ahead. Anticipate a shock if there is an explosion. Sparks display your bright ideas, which will take you to extraordinary places.

Fish: Fish in clear water reveal good financial news. A fish gasping for air means you may feel like a fish out of water because you are working against your best interests. If you throw the fish back into the water, your emotional recovery is at hand. Fishing shows you are looking for something. If you catch a fish, you will get your wish. If not, it is unlikely that you will get what you want soon.

Flag: To see a flag flying or being raised means a personal victory and that approval of your beliefs and opinions is coming. A lowered flag points to a decline in your success.

Flood: A surge of emotions may overwhelm you or someone close to you.

Flowers: Flowers represent your own soul and seasons. Love will flower and bloom in your heart. Remember and follow your heart by evoking good flower memories from the past. Pure love will grow and present beautiful changes and natural pleasures in the spring. To pull the roots out of the soil while picking flowers means that you risk jeopardizing your own happiness for someone or something unworthy of your time and attention. A flower arrangement reveals that you are well balanced mentally, physically, spiritually, and emotionally. A bouquet forecasts a love affair or acclaim for you. A withered or discarded bouquet or flower represents a broken relationship and disappointment.

Carnation: Genuine love is in the air.

Chrysanthemum: There will be news concerning your mother.

Daffodil: Someone may trifle with your affections.

Daisy: Your innocence is inspirational to one who holds you in his or her thoughts.

Geraniums: One you love may reject you.

Lavender: Someone is devotedly yours.

Lilac: In the spring, someone from the past will return.

Marigolds: You will prosper in the next twelve months.

Orchids: Passion may devour you.

Pansies: Someone thinks of you night and day.

Primroses: Someone will openly confide in you.

Roses: True, eternal love will appear. Someone will be forever in your heart.

Tulips: Someone will declare undying love to you.

Food: Food on a table is a sign that you will feast in spiritual nourishment and faith, contentment and success. Unhappiness with food means discontentment. Food shopping in a dream means you seek fulfillment.

Bread: Expect an unexpected stroke of good luck that is a foundation for future happiness.

Cake: You will receive an afternoon invitation, from old friends if you see a fruit cake and from relatives if the cake is iced. You will be more fortunate than you anticipate in a situation you are apprehensive about.

Cheese: You will make financial gains.

Cookies: Sweet cookies suggest a love of life shared with friends. Crackers indicate a sour attitude to people and life generally. People with religious faiths dreaming of wafer biscuits may feel they need reassurance from their church.

Eggs: You will amass material possessions.

Fish: An inspirational flash of insight will come to you.

Juice: You are going to receive a boost of light-hearted happiness through good news that gives you an occasion to look forward to.

Meat: A short phase of ill health may follow.

Nuts: You will "crack" a dilemma.

It is said that money will be given to you if you spot a frog.

Olives: You will put yourself in an honorable position.

Rice: A long-cherished desire is about to be fulfilled.

Salad: You have a conscience about a healthy diet. Spring and summer will be happy seasons.

Salt: Pleasure is in store.

Sugar: A warning not to place your trust in a sweet-talker.

Tea: You have pleasant friendships to look forward to.

Forest:
You may not be able to "see the forest for the trees" or realize someone is deceiving you if you are lost or afraid in the forest. To be happy there shows you deeply understand your journey through life.

[67]

Frog:
Your life will "metamorphose" for the better. Something or someone is about to change you as the frog changed into a prince.

Fruits:
Your labors will come to fruition and you will satisfy your sensual, earthly desires. You may hear of a pregnancy.

Apple: Your thirst for knowledge will be quenched.

Apricot: Expect modest success in the immediate future.

Banana: Bananas are phallic symbols. Men are on your mind.

Make a wish when you taste a fruit for the first time in the season.

Grapes: An advance may be followed by a decline.

Lemon: Current happiness may be transient.

Melon: Your delicate situation may easily be spoiled.

Orange: Being spherical in shape, an orange represents your whole mind; the segments reveal the multiplicity of your wholeness.

Peach: You will be granted a special gift.

Pears: You will have a loving relationship, and will marry if you pick pears.

Pineapple: You will travel soon.

Plum: A shortcut to prosperity may not pay worthwhile dividends.

Strawberries: Your wish will come true.

[68]

~*G*~

Garden: Your consciousness is represented by a garden. An unusually beautiful garden with sparkling flowers and vividly colored wildlife means you have seen a heavenly realm and returned with the knowledge that higher forces are helping you. If the garden is of an earthly type but lovely, a talent or project you cultivate will grow and mature. You should continue down any noticeable path, but if it leads to dark trees, which represent your subconscious, someone may be leading you "up the garden path," where you will lose your way. A scruffy garden foreshadows loneliness and solitude, but hanging baskets show that you will be radiating a visible new happiness.

Ghost: You may feel haunted by an elusive memory but you may also be currently wasting your time putting effort into the people or home around where the ghost appeared.

Gift: You will encounter a fair stranger if you receive a gift from someone of the opposite sex, and a dark stranger if it came from someone of your own sex. Romantic enjoyment and a glamorous infatuation lie ahead. If you wrap or give a gift, you will soon be giving of yourself to someone appreciative.

[69]

Glass: You may feel fearful and unprotected in facing someone or something directly, and you may be right to feel this way, for timing is important for the removal of barriers. However, something that is delayed may not be able to be put off forever. To look through spectacles means that you should look at your situation thoughtfully.

Glass or Drinking Goblet: To drink from a glass means you will be drinking from a new spring of happiness. An ardent and passionate romance or celebration will follow. A broken glass means shattered illusions, a broken love affair, and a broken heart. The next lover you meet may be potentially harmful.

Gold: Supernatural intelligence is an elusive treasure you possess. Golden thoughts spinning around your mind when woven together should bring warm rays of sunshine into your life with a wealth of happiness and financial riches.

Guitar: You may have a romantic flirtation in which someone is playing with your heartstrings. A broken string foreshadows a broken heart.

Gun: Your plans are likely to collapse if a gun is being pointed toward you. If you point the gun even at a bull's-eye target, it is a sign that you are about to commit a foolish indiscretion. To hear a gunshot is a warning of insincerity, arguments, and potential harm.

~H~

Hair: Lustrous hair is a sign of good health and financial prosperity. Long hair means you will travel far. Falling hair or baldness foreshadows slight ill health and disillusionment followed by renewed determination. To see your own or another's hair being colored or styled reveals a change in you that is good or bad according to whether you like or dislike the style or color.

Hair holds the psychic energy of its owner. To have a lock of someone's hair is

Hammer: You may buy, auction, or become involved in collecting valuable items, but someone you know socially may put pressure on you to sell a hard-earned or treasured item.

Hat: You may be asked to keep a secret or think it best to keep your own privacy. Wearing a hat shows you may be given an enduring promotion. To lose a hat means you will be discredited. To buy a new hat precedes news of a wedding.

Headphones: You may be deaf to someone who is trying to get a message across to you loud and clear. Ruminating on a recent conversation, you will discover another's words speak volumes by revealing his or her psyche. Understanding this puts you in a higher position of knowing what motivates that person.

[71]

Heart: You are the center of someone's attention and will experience a strong force that draws you closer. The light of love will illuminate your life with a warm and eternal glow. Selfish love will be easily discarded because you will know the difference in your heart.

Herbs: Good people, friends, and relatives are represented by dreams of herbs. Social encounters may be bittersweet. The more pleasant the herbs, the happier the company you keep will be. The more leaves, the more numerous your social acquaintances.

to have a supernatural link with that person.

Hill: To climb a hill in a dream is encouragement to keep climbing. Nothing that happens to you in life will deter you from reaching the pinnacle and winning. Once there, you will have a panoramic view offering many choices. Within the next year to year and a half, you should find yourself in a much more elevated situation.

Hole: A hole in a dream represents a gateway between this world and the next. Not only is your personality developing, but so too is a project or plan that could give you a new lease on life. Higher knowledge will result from sorrows that are now past.

[72]

Hospital: You are recovering from a psychological disappointment or a physical illness. A time of rest and recuperation is forecast.

House: Your heart is symbolized by a house. The outside of a house represents your personality and physical appearance. The roof relates to your head, and the top story to your mind and willpower. The ground floor and basement signify your intuition and talents, especially the kitchen, because it is there that food is changed from one state to another by cooking. The stairs link stages of your spirit and mind. Concern about a particular room relates to the corresponding part of your psyche or that of a person you were dream-

The first time a visitor enters your house, he or she can make a wish. You can make a wish

ing of. A cabin shows that you may be happy with simplicity for a time and might sacrifice material comforts for your own sincere feelings. You may renounce short-term happiness or profits for long-term gain. If you are single, someone special may be about to enter your life.

Housework: Doing housework reveals a desire
to be organized and shows that you are actually putting your "house's" mind, spirit, and body in order. Doing the laundry shows that you are getting rid of the old and preparing for something new. To be vacuuming shows there will be no delay in your success.

Husband: If you dream of having a husband, you
will, but not for some time.

~I~

Ice: Ice divides, with your conscious above it and
your soul below. A decision or choice that has until now been frozen or put on ice needs resolving. Knowing that you can see what is above but not below may help you to not take a chance by skating on thin ice.

Injection: If you are happy about being injected
then you will receive a boost by attracting the right help and good fortune from an outside source. If not, you may be mixing with harmful people.

upon entering another person's home for the first time.

Insects: You will easily transcend minor irritations and petty annoyances that may arrive or perhaps be solved in early spring.

Ants: Prosperity will follow after strenuous endeavors.

Beetles: Domestic troubles are forecast.

Bees and Beehives: Wisdom and financial wealth will increase.

Butterflies: You will have a new flirtatious love affair and, one day, a happy marriage.

Fleas: Since fleas suck blood, this dream reveals that you are already in trouble.

Moths: Moths, because they eat clothes, reveal financial problems.

[74]

Internet: A great idea that may be the focal point of a reunion is winging its way to you through the ether. Your life will suddenly encompass a whole new understanding. An instant attraction, perhaps romantic or family love, will lead you out of seclusion into a big world where you will encounter interesting people, embark on up-to-date activities, and lay past differences to rest. You will transcend a difficult situation and two hearts will unite.

If you put a shiny new coin in your purse on the first of January and keep it throughout the year, you will never be poor.

~ J ~

Jail: Things that you feel you must answer to are the faults of others coupled with your own naïveté. Be careful in whom you place your trust. If you are behaving illegally, this dream acts as a warning to stop.

Jewelry: If you give jewelry, you are expressing love. To receive it means you will flourish financially and become wealthy through superior intelligence. You may gather gems of spiritual truths and intuition. A precious love affair may begin. If diamonds are involved, you will both be faithful to each other. Earrings mean a lover you wish to hear from will make contact, unless the earrings are broken. Also, if they are difficult to wear you will have to wait a while. A necklace means that a love link will begin a chain reaction. A broken chain represents broken love links. A bracelet reveals that bonds of love and friendship will be strengthened; it also forecasts marriage. Pearls may mean wisdom through tears, rubies mean mental stability, emeralds signify constancy in love, and sapphires peace.

Judge: If you stand before a judge, you may be intuitively judging your own actions and conscience or having judgment passed from the spirit world. To be ruled as innocent means to put your mind at peace. Good fortune will continue, because your inward feelings ascend to what fate has assigned. Changing your ways through good advice can avert trouble.

Jungle: A jungle represents your subconscious. Your instincts are telling you that you are doing something right if you enjoy the jungle. If, however, you are lost or fearful, someone may attempt to trick or pressure you into behaving out of character.

~*K*~

Keys: You will be crossing a mysterious threshold and unlocking a new door to your destiny. You are being offered a spiritual key to your soul and the gate of immortality. You may also close doors, because you possess the key of choice. Two keys are love keys, because two people share the same home. Three keys reveal precious rooms in your heart, soul, and mind where love, inspiration, and memories live. To find a key promises that you will discover beautiful, sparkling treasures even after great difficulties. To drop a key means you will move or travel.

King: The king is a male in your psyche. Magic and supernatural powers will bring you a precious marriage made in heaven that begins with a love affair. Supreme consciousness will crown you king by merit of your royal virtues. Honesty, sound judgment, and self-control link you to the ethereal. If the king is ill, you risk losing love. You will instead focus on haunting shadows.

Kiss: Kissing someone you love may be wishful thinking, but it may also be that you will kiss that person if you are likely to meet. To kiss someone you dislike shows that your thoughts go beyond your outward aversion to see a likeable person underneath the surface. Kissing a famous pop star, VIP, or someone unobtainable is more likely to be a desire than a premonition.

Kitchen: If the kitchen is clean and pleasant, family emotions are good. If the kitchen is unclean, you or a relative lack superficial understanding, but beneath the surface, love presides. A lover will introduce you to his or her family. You will be welcomed into their hearts and they will find a home in yours.

Knife: A long knife shows your spiritual talents will lead you to conquer great career heights but not without crusade or sacrifice of time. A short-bladed knife reveals that you are not cutting through what holds you back from achievement. Scissors forecast an argument as well as consciously cutting something harmful out of your life.

Knot: Love is a tie, an endless knot whose links cannot be broken even by death. You will be in contact with someone distant and may know him or her your whole life long if the connection is pure. To undo or cut a knot shows your existence will lack luster if you do not find and achieve your life purpose.

Lace: Beauty and elegance are entering your life if you dream about lace. You may soon be able to enjoy a lengthy spell of relaxation, a vacation, or the glow of achievement during which you taste the finer and more delicate quality of life.

[78] **Ladder:** You are gradually ascending a phase or project, and the number of steps may be relevant to days, weeks, months, or years. You are making a breakthrough by looking vertically to your goal and by taking the right steps to attain the world you see.

Lake: A lake is a supernatural psychic veil reflecting a mirror of self-contemplation. If you dream of a lake in tranquility, an answer will become transparently clear by casting sunlight into the depth of the water where your soul is deeply rooted. Past and future can then be leveled and united. You will find the fluid connection from deep roots mirrored by branches that are roots of future growth. The revelation dawns first in your conscious but is felt in your soul. What you reflect conjures wonderful imaginings to be followed. Reaching heaven, thoughts transcend all that may dampen or dilute your rising spirit. Transient pools require a quick decision and denote a quick change that can be eternally and purely yours.

Letter: Your reaction to the letter is significant heralding good or bad news. Communication is winging its way to you, perhaps from a source you are anticipating to hear news from. A letter may suggest that your dream will come true on the day that a special true-life letter arrives. Alphabet letters display that your dream is plainly trying to spell something out to you. But alphabet letters may also relate to the initial of a person's name in your life.

Lights: Higher deities are trying to make you see the light in a current predicament. The color of the light may be significant as to how you face your future, perhaps with a different and lighter view. August and September will be enlightening.

Lightning and Thunder: Thunder reveals that supreme, creative energy is shaking up you or others. A new beginning that is superior to past patterns will invigorate and recharge your energy and everyday activities. An illuminating thought is a seed of clairvoyant brightness that destroys past thunderclouds. New energies entering your life need careful handling to avoid troubles. You may shock someone who sees you with the very person that he or she fancies.

Line: If you dream of standing in a line waiting for someone or something, be patient, for your turn will come. Where you stand in line may be significant in how long your aim will take to achieve. People in front of you may represent those you have to pass in order to succeed.

Lovers: You will ultimately find true love and recognize your soul mate when you have a feeling or an awareness that pops into your mind. A current separation may lead to kissing and making up.

~ *M* ~

Machines: You will be given credit for productive achievements that have set a rhythm for your future movement. To keep matters running smoothly you may be assimilating what you understand to avoid hurting someone's feelings. To break or see a broken machine precedes a broken work relationship.

Makeup: Wearing makeup reveals that by making the most of your inherent charms, you are and will continue to be the person that you like and have aspired to become. To buy makeup unveils that an imminent transformation is about to occur in your life. To see another wearing or applying makeup means there is more depth to that person or to you than appears at first glance.

Man: A man presents a conflict and a solution to your emotions, thoughts, and ideas. In analogies and symbols a man may be awakening you to see an aggressive or masculine part of yourself you may not have known existed. He is a private messenger of good or bad news of a personal or worldwide nature. Expect a meeting of opposites to arise, knowing that friendliness will result.

Map: You will discover new opportunities that will be far afield if the map is large. You may move locations for a short or long spell. You may be mapping out your life and making your mark. The condition and color of the map reveal how smoothly your life journey will run.

[81]

Massage: A soothing spell is forecast during which you can happily forget your worries. If you are being massaged you will hear good news from someone who wishes to pamper you. If someone else is having a massage, your good news will also cheer someone close.

Medicine: Minor problems are being resolved. To give medicine shows that you should forget retribution and be healed.

Message: To receive a message is a sure sign that one is on the way that will make you happy or sad. If you are laughing in the dream, you will laugh when you receive your waking-life message and may receive an unexpected gift.

Mirror: Expect flattery from a potential lover who will consciously highlight your imagination. You may contemplate your subconscious and reflect what is visible to your physical and clairvoyant sight. Your past and future are now coming into focus. A hand mirror symbolizes that you will find the truth by not looking at things from a one-sided viewpoint.

Money: If you found money in your dream, you may be entangled in difficulties. If you lose money, you will succeed in your plans. If you count money, you will gain money. If you win the lottery, ask for the numbers to be given in your sleep, then use them in your waking life.

Monsters: You fear your own impulses. However, you have every reason to be fearless if you are strong willed and sensible. Your own light can triumph over the darkness inside and outside yourself.

Moon: Love is growing. Someone you think does not love you really does. Small signs will become visibly stronger. The light of love will grow out of night gloom, and you will meet. Your relationship may grow and mature and reshape your life. The moon phase may be significant as an indication of time when love develops. You have many emotionally enriching moments to look forward to. A full moon shows how many unreliable friends you have, since their light disappears with the shade.

Mountain: Matters of opposing opinions may reach a high peak where you prove you can be more than you imagined. Great generosity surrounds you. Climbing a mountain shows you are aiming for something great; descending precedes a decline in confidence or circumstance.

Museum: Your past and future will inspire a meeting with someone of similar mind. From that day your efforts and talent will help you to ascend from your well-trodden path and to progress along another. The person you meet will be someone you feel grateful to when your directions divide.

Music: You will call the harmonious tune for someone striking a chord in your heart with romantic overtures. A marriage may quickly occur. You may be taking a lover's leap in the same direction of high or low musical tones.

Names: Your soul magnetically reflects on someone on your wavelength. Power lies in names. Names called mean something personal to you. Names may be puns or synonyms.

Newspaper: You may very soon hear startling news from a distance. To wrap something in newspaper means a house move, as well as a happy reunion with an old acquaintance.

Night: The darkest hour is always before dawn. A dream of night promises that a bright new day is dawning for you. However, night also represents ignorance that dwells in subconscious darkness instead of seeing daylight and the promise of a new day.

Nudity: Your inward expressions are finding freedom. You will be noticing little things about someone you have met and like, the color of his or her eyes, shape of the hands, and what he or she wears, because you are falling in love. Romance and spiritual attraction, physical beauty and lust play in your thoughts.

Nurse: You are a caring person and may become a professional nurse. You are telling yourself to take gentle care of your health or to have a checkup. A dream of a nurse may also represent someone you know and are experiencing difficulties with. You may come to the rescue of someone who needs help.

Ocean: A deep ocean represents your soul, where waves of emotion stir. White foam on waves shows that your thoughts and emotions are pure. A calm ocean reveals inner serenity. Large waves and a high tide mean that turbulent passion, yours or someone else's, may overwhelm you. Your reaction to the ocean, whether it is fear or happiness, implies that you possess the same feelings in waking life. If you are laughing in the dream you will soon be riding high on the crest of a wave.

Office: In the future, you may work in an office or change your occupation or business skills to a new line of work leading to success. You may be telling yourself to become better organized. What happens in the office is significant to how you should react to and streamline your career.

Oven: You may be yearning for motherly love and reassurance from higher spiritual forces that give definite feelings of being looked after and kept warm. Rest assured that one of your desires is a recipe for success that will nourish your needs and regenerate your faith.

Package: A surprise is coming, and an opportunity will soon arrive in which you may be able to remove barriers between you and the object of your desire or affection. A happy turn of events will come when you least expect it.

Palace: Following your dreams and heart in work or love will take you to palatial homes and beautiful locations. Your thoughts are already connected to great beauty. A new sphere of activity, better than any you have known before, is about to unfold.

Park: You may be pleasing others rather than yourself, bringing superficial rather than deep fulfillment. Swings and merry-go-rounds leave you questioning where your true happiness lies. A dizzy relationship may be short-lived and short-loved.

Party: A social whirl may sweep you off your feet. To refuse a party invitation precedes a period of loneliness.

Path: A new path of activity may be opening up for you. A clear-cut path means you will quickly and easily reach your destination. A winding path reveals that your path ahead will take odd turns. An overgrown path means past and future difficulties will slow your progress. To lose your way and find it again means that you will find your way in life. The nature of what you walk on is also significant, for it may designate a smooth or rough journey and a specific season.

Pen/Pencil: You will be communicating in writing with someone. If the ink color is light, good news will come. If dark, expect meaningful or serious correspondence. A broken pen or pencil means a problem may be halved. Perhaps someone acting as a mediator will set things down clearly in black and white. A signature is personal to what you sign and give approval to. If you are uncomfortable, the message is to not commit.

Perfume: Something sweet is in the air. An instant emotional level will magnetically draw you to someone at the moment you meet. The attraction will pervade your mind and theirs, and you will gradually meet again and again until you are bound together as friends or lovers. Nostalgic feelings will link both of you.

Photographs: You may be seeing your future. You are also seeing your soul, because a photo is an image and double of yourself. A photo torn in half represents a broken relationship, not necessarily your own. The theme of the photo shows a past or future event.

[87]

Piano: Romantic bliss is entering your life. If you enjoy the melody of the music, romance may lead to marital happiness. A situation may land on a high or low note, according to the tune.

Picnic: Someone will show you a simple kindness, bringing a bright ray of sunshine into your heart. You will appreciate the fresh air of freedom in simple pleasures. A dull phase is ending, allowing you to breathe freely and embrace a brighter, more carefree future.

Plants: Your plans and projects are about to flourish. The plants may symbolize the season when this will happen. You are becoming happier, more prosperous,

and more worldly, but nature cannot be rushed.
Faith and patience are easier when you follow your
dreams and the natural flow of time.

Playing Cards: Gambling, playing, winning, or
losing reveal the future outcome of a scenario you are
currently handling. If gambling, the risk is high and
you are aiming at making changes by taking small
risks. Being the player, you can choose to change the
outcome by playing your cards according to your better
judgment.

President: This fatherly figure represents how you
view your father. You realize that you are not totally
free from restriction and that even your soul lives by
moral codes. By playing by the rules you succeed in
having the freedom to be yourself.

Prize: You are going to be a winner of merit. You
could be awarded a prize or receive a metaphorical tro-
phy. An ambition carries a cosmic seal of approval.

Purse or Pocketbook: An important future
occasion could be a noteworthy career or social turning
point. It urges you to take notice of imminent events
that may lead to valuable contacts.

Puzzle: You may be faced with a dilemma that you
will be able to solve. The nature of the puzzle in the
dream relates to your conundrum. No puzzle will be

unsolvable because you will follow your intuition, which leads to the jigsaw pieces' slotting into place at the right time.

Queen: If you dream of a queen accompanying a king, someone touches your heart and will bring eternal rescue. Visible love light results from the blending of spiritual coincidence and a marriage of soul and consciousness. When you achieve victory you will be crowned with golden glory. You are at the heart of a sweetheart's existence. One who truly loves you will place you in an exalted position, strongly balancing eternal love and worldly security. To dine with a queen precedes a rise in status within months and a feast of happiness in elite, convivial company.

[89]

Race: You are competing to win, and how you fare in the dream race reveals your progress. To win a race means that you will win in a difficult situation. How long the race has yet to run may be shown by a lap. Falling behind shows that you fear failure, not that you will fail to win.

Radio: What you listen to is indicative of pleasing or displeasing news that you will soon hear. You will very quickly discover that your extrasensory perception is tuned into someone's intentions.

Rain: Your plans are about to burst into life. Growing spiritual influences inspiring personal growth promise rich fulfillment of your endeavors. You may need patience and perseverance before success appears.

Rainbow: Your soul's knowledge of your past is displaying potential brilliance. Treasured, heaven-sent opportunities are about to radiate colorful hues that bring happy changes. You are inspired to transcend your troubles by crossing a bridge, linking your lower and higher selves.

Razor: Keep your wits sharply about you. You may just avoid a dangerous situation. Delicate business dealings are about to occur.

Restaurant: A plush restaurant means your health and career aims are being well nourished.

Ring: You may hear of a birth, death, or marriage. This dream also means that your life is in sync with the eternal, universal life cycle and will naturally become whole. In the fullness of time there will be no area of your life that remains unfulfilled. A lover may propose. If you are single, a new sweetheart is about to appear.

To lose a ring or see it drop from your finger means you will lose a love, but a new beginning will continue.

River: Creative powers flowing through you are leading you out into the mainstream of life. A small river shows things may flow sparingly at first on your ride of destiny. Trouble in a river refers to difficulties that hinder your advance. You will make progress but may sense regret for what you leave behind.

Robot: You may be behaving in a robotic fashion, without your heart being in what you do, or you may feel that you are working too mechanically.

[91]

Rocks: Your foundations are permanently secure. By taking one step at a time, you will find that a slippery situation will become rock solid. A minor problem will disappear into perspective.

Rocket: International news of an outbreak of war or natural disaster may follow.

Rock Star: You will be in the spotlight and have many admirers. You could achieve fame if it is your ambition.

Room: You will be making room for new people in your life. The nature of any room exhibits your thoughts. Windows show understanding, because light shines in through them. A closed door shows you may be keeping to yourself. If the door is open, you are openly communicating your inner sentiments. Conversations in rooms relate to concealed or evident attachments to certain people.

Rope: You may be making new connections with intelligent people or actively committing yourself to an enduring course of study or a project that cannot be achieved overnight. Your accomplishment will express the essence of your nature and securely bind you to your destined niche in life.

Ruins: You possibly fear impending ruin that may not necessarily materialize. You are urging yourself to keep building the foundations of your future.

Running: You are speedily getting to where you want to be but wish to get there sooner. If you are being chased, evil may approach you, and you need to be rid of a situation.

~ *S* ~

Satellite: You are a satellite. Someone you have met is about to orbit you but only if you keep quiet and respond infrequently. Those who are not destined for you will find nothing to cling to and will slip away. Your destiny is fixed in your mind and cannot be shaken.

Fine weather on January 22 is a good omen: "It is a token

School: Being happy in school reveals self-confidence. You are about to receive praise for past efforts. A gift is coming to you. To be unhappy reveals guilt, perhaps connected to childhood. You have learned an invaluable lesson that should help you face the big, wide world.

Scooter: You are making a speedy transition from dependence to independence. It may be some time before you are in a true position of strength that will eventually take you far in a much safer position.

Seasons: The season that you dream about is one you are looking forward to, one that will bring good luck and a change for the better. Mists reveal that your partially obscured future is fusing. Clouds represent your passing moods.

[93]

> *Summer:* A time is arriving for you to take a leisurely vacation and to do all the things you have wanted to. You may be socializing in new company as well as traveling. Your fruits will ripen if well tended, and the sun will shine for you.
> *Autumn:* You will be saving long-term time and energy by organizing yourself. The vestiges of the old will become the basis for something new.
> *Winter:* Family relationships will be strengthened when you share what is yours. An opportunity

bright and clear,
Of prosperous weather
all the year."

will arrive for you to rid yourself of unwanted
people or situations.

Spring: Spring brings the potential for a new
sweetheart and a loving romance. It is also a new
beginning with a project, team, or sports interest.

Seed: Your wish will come true, and you will get your
desire. You are strong in wealth, health, love, and happiness. Seeds you have sown will take root, flourish,
and ripen, bearing fruits for many years to come. The
first week of September and last week of May will
be significantly pleasing to you, bringing a reunion,
a lover's meeting, or a fresh start that makes you happy.

[94]

Sex: With this dream you reveal maternal instincts
and may be discovering a male aspect of your psyche.
Making love with someone who is not your partner
shows you have reservations about your partner and
feel dissatisfied with him or her.

Shark: If the sharks are close to the water's surface,
visible competition may confront you. Competition is
concealed if the sharks are in deep sea. Snapping sharks
reveal that a dangerous situation is fast approaching
and that you are wise to play it safe.

Shell: You are picking up jewels from your soul when
holding a shell. A wonderful happening is about to
rush into your life, for you are going to find someone
or something that deserves wonder. Your intuition will
guide how you react to the momentous event.

Ship: Someone passionate wishes to seduce you in a sea of love. A sudden change will steer your destiny on a new and joyous course that brings rich rewards. Your triumph in surfing the waves and discovering new oceans relies on balancing your emotional soul in perspective with new material horizons that beckon you ashore to safety.

Shoes: Liberty and freedom are your desires. Shoes symbolize female sex organs, and feet your soul. You may be leaving signals for your sweetheart or a potential lover to find. Shoes or boots that are too big warn against dangerous behavior. Scruffy shoes indicate financial hardship ahead. To lose a heel means you will lose a friend. To wear new shoes means that you are taking the right steps to meet your match and will be stepping out in bright new company.

[95]

Shopping Mall: You guard your heart's sentiments in the glare of bright and valuable opportunities. If a shop is closed or you have no money, you feel your desires are unattainable. To be lost expresses fear of being unable to find a way through a current situation.

Sign: You may be changing direction and an old lifestyle. The significance of something that attracted your attention may have been overlooked. You are wise to read the signs people send out.

Singer: An opportunity will arrive for you to express the sentiments of your heart, and someone will be singing your praises. If the voice is melodious and the tune harmonious, your happiness will be shared by many who know you. Even a sad song may precede good news. You may be about to meet a new lover.

Sky: Clear blue skies mean happiness, and clouds mean that your troubles will quickly evaporate. The sky is the limit, so aim high; you are destined for major achievements.

Snake: Strength is on your side, giving you a new lease on life to achieve a treasured goal. Your health is returning after sickness. Romantic feelings could tempt you to physical pleasures you may feel sinful about.

Snow: Your pure emotions may be frozen, but a fresh start is about to appear. You will meet a lover who melts your heart.

Space: A chaotic situation is suddenly going to become clear in your heart. To be on the right-hand side of space shows that sunshine will appear in a situation when you take action. To be on or see the left-hand side in space means an emotional situation, making you introverted and obstructing clear vision. Space straight ahead reveals that a new phase will truly transform your future outlook.

Speech: You will be passing on good news that is about to bring emotional and physical happiness. You may in the future speak to an audience if you are giving or hearing a speech. The substance of the speech relates to the area of your life that will put you on stage or on show.

Spiders: Even if you fear spiders, this dream is a sign of wealth. A spider's web reveals that you are creatively weaving the threads of your destiny around a central ambition. The future you spin is imaginative, psychic, and beautiful.

Star: Your wish will come true. Bright, spiritual light is shining on you. Your mood is rising upward, as is every area of your life. You are going to be learning and teaching in many ways. Your destiny is favorable and happy because you have faith. Many bright stars will supernaturally twinkle in moments of personal darkness, linking and creating a brighter constellation in your heavenly life. A comet brings a message of chaos in your affairs.

[97]

Storm: If you have this dream, you may be reminding yourself to be careful and safe. Difficulties are dissolving, and a sudden, unexpected change is about to free you from oppression. You may have to find inner strength to forgive people who have wronged you. Whoever tries to cling to you will let go when you stop thinking about him or her. When the air has cleared you will blossom by not dwelling on your own or another's mistakes.

Subway: Trouble in a subway may relate to a trauma or difficulty of being born, but it may be a warning to beware of traveling alone late at night.

Sun: If you are facing the sun, like a shadow your problems are beyond you. If the sun is behind you and you are facing the shadow, a problem is not yet fully solved. A sunset means an end. Hot sun signifies intelligence.

~*T*~

Table: To be alone at a table reveals arrogance and loneliness. Being with another at a table shows that a relationship you long for will develop into an intimate meeting where you and a sweetheart will exchange loving words.

Tattoo: To be tattooed means you deeply and unchangeably wish to sacrifice higher knowledge and better understanding to a stamp that is the brand of an influence alien to you.

Teacher: You may be about to learn a lesson or suddenly feel responsibility being taken away from you.

Someone or an event may make you look at things differently. Having a crush on a teacher shows that your rational sensibilities are being aroused and connected with your emotions.

Telephone: You will receive a message concerning lucky career and business news. In love, a promising phone call on its way will take you by surprise.

Telescope: By focusing on what is far and bringing it near and into perspective, you can attain an ambition or heartfelt desire. Attention to detail is particularly important for your success. Look far ahead into the long term to view the winning picture in your mind. Someone may be prying into your private affairs.

[99]

Television: Watching alone precedes an important event you will think about for months to come. Viewing in company means someone or something may be attempting to block communication and the natural flow of events.

Tent: Your feelings may be divided. A situation is temporary and changing. Your desire to get close to nature will strengthen your resolve for security and stability.

Tennis: You will attain social happiness. The ball is in your court. You will serve, ace, and score in love. Your mental and physical stamina will ensure that you play for game, set, and match.

Test: A challenge you desire is about to occur, and you may fear your performance. An academic test reveals you lack confidence in your intelligence. A physical test of weights, that you doubt your physical strength. However, you will survive a testing time no matter what.

Theater: Dreams play charades, as you are the player who acts out ideas. All the actors in the theater may be parts of your personality that your soul sees you play. A character represents a part of your psyche that you identify with: a professor is your intelligence, a loose woman your sexuality, a doctor your healing qualities. Actors may also represent the roles of people you know, so the theme is relevant. Someone you long to see is most certainly going to put in an appearance. You may attain great success as an actor if that is your ambition.

[100]

Toys: You will meet someone whose love and affection for you will be strong. To be unhappy with toys means someone may tempt you to play with life, and you will fail to achieve the genuine love and marriage prize you deserve. Not wanting to waste time, you will then have the choice not to play with those who do not love or respect you.

Treasure: Your soul is an elusive treasure, as is your intuition. A past suffering is a memory that heightens your self-awareness, creating a moral choice and a step toward progress. Many wonderful gems will sparkle in your life. You will go to unique places and meet enriching people who will become precious to you.

Tree: A tree may represent your soul or a loved one's. The point is that you are being drawn to people by connective roots. The tree's roots are your foundation and past, the trunk your social life and the present, and the branches your higher self and future. Your attention may be drawn to a particular area, but all are connected, so the context might be important. Bare trees represent a phase of isolation and recovery. Lush trees mean your life is about to blossom or bear fruit; the season of the tree's growth may designate when.

[101]

Tunnel: You may be entering the tunnel of love. Being scared means you sense a difficult passage; it may connect to a stressful birth or childhood experience. Sensing light at the end of a tunnel shows you have an enlightened mind and are entering into a bright new day.

Umbrella: A fatherly person is keeping you safe. A closed umbrella shows an upturn in your financial affairs, so there will be no rainy day to save for in the foreseeable future. To let your guard down and lose an umbrella may precede misfortune. An umbrella pointing down and standing partially open means your rainy day is finally over. Expect a lucky shower of love, family, career, and money wishes to come true.

Utensils: You have many potentialities at your fingertips, but they must become active tools to achieve your desires. New opportunities arriving should not be overlooked.

HOTEL ROYAL·NICE

~*V*~

Vacation: You will receive an invitation to go on vacation. Sunshine and happiness are about to brighten your days ahead.

Valley: Your deep thoughts are creatively developing your future. Your life may take an unusual turn.

Vegetables: Planting, tending, and eating vegetables precede a happy but intense love affair. Spoiled vegetables mean a relationship is deteriorating.

> *Beans:* Your feminine side is enduring.
> *Broccoli:* Your social life is about to flourish.
> *Carrots:* You are thinking of someone's ardor.
> *Mushrooms:* A love affair may be transient.
> *Onions:* You may shed tears of heartache.
> *Peas:* Your sweetheart's family and friends will adore you.
> *Potato:* A lover will stand the test of time.

It is said to be an unlucky omen

Pumpkin: A sign of oneness; you and your partner may become united.

Tomato: Your success is fragile and dependent on
your actions.

Video:
You may revisit loving or haunting experiences
over and over again in your mind, but because you are
in control of the switch to avoid allowing history to
repeat itself, you can fast-forward and begin anew.
You may reunite with someone from your past or meet
someone with remarkably familiar idiosyncrasies.

Video Game:
Playing a video game means your
mind and willpower have a higher, winning perspective.
You are about to achieve a great victory.

[103]

Volcano:
A volatile situation is about to erupt. The
tension that can already be felt is a warning to get away
from the danger.

Walking:
A leisurely walk means you will stroll
through life in the immediate future. Difficulty walking is an expression of problems in your path. To watch
another person walk reveals a lack of energy to see
your plans through to completion.

to drop food you are
putting into your mouth.

Wall: You are rising above barriers that have held you back. Higher forces are helping your efforts by removing obstacles that have blocked your progress.

Washing: Washing reveals that you may be preparing to cleanse and sacrifice for a higher cause and purpose that takes you onward and upward. You will be getting rid of the old and introducing the new.

Water: A negative situation is being washed away and cleansed. Clear water means that your emotions are tranquil and clear. Muddy water means disputes and danger. Hot water is a sign of danger. Washing in water indicates a fresh start, and drinking water happiness. Water in dreams does not always feel wet.

[104]

Web Site/www: You will be able to manage anything you put your mind to. Having a multitude of choices at your fingertips, you will find the right connections that open up a whole new world for you. The world is your oyster.

Wedding: You will receive a wedding invitation. Romance in the air is bringing you a sweet love affair.

Whale: A situation you embrace may turn into its opposite for a while, but you will emerge stronger.

Wheel: Plans and ideas set in motion are about to gain momentum. A new cycle will begin, taking you away from a difficult passage of time.

Wife: To dream that you are someone's wife is an omen that you will marry. The groom in the dream may represent the character traits you desire in your life partner. To dream of someone else being a wife means marriage for you will come after career happiness.

Window: You will be viewing life in a much happier frame of mind. New opportunities that beckon could lead you on a path that continues into the distance of time. A closed window reveals that you may be closing your mind to potential bright new horizons. A situation similar to the one that has ended may begin.

Wine: Red wine signifies youth and eternal life because red is the color of blood, but it also means sacrifice in the sense that youthfulness is transitory. One happy situation may soon be given up for something new. White wine brings a message of celebrations in happy company where your confidence will be boosted.

[105]

Wings: Wings on any being reveal that you will soar to heavenly heights by way of your spiritual imagination. You are about to experience an intelligent victory that becomes enlightened by seeing the unseen. You may meet the love of your life, and peace will prevail.

Witch: Love, mystery, and magic are casting happy spells on your life. You know that magical forces are working in your favor, confirmed by your strong sixth sense of intuition, which combines your physical and spiritual senses of sight, hearing, smell, taste, and touch. You can see and shape your future any way you wish. Halloween may be a significant time for love. When you allow the psyche of another to work on you, consequential knowledge reveals how to get your wish.

Woman: The woman in your dream may be a wiser part of your own nature, expressing that you have a life mission to accomplish. Your attention may be drawn to a future result or event open to new options. If you like the woman, she shows that you possess perfection in bringing out the best qualities of your soul mate. If the woman is monstrous, beware: someone damaging may try to divert you from your life purpose.

Wreath: You will lay your grief for relatives to rest. Grief will give birth to a happy reunion in which memories germinate future love that grows and blooms. The link of love is not broken by death but deepened and raised to a heavenly sphere of reciprocation.

Writing: You will receive written proof of a loving person's sentiments for you. Reading short or long paragraphs or pages represents a period of time that you may spend in the company of the person of your dreams.

It is believed that you will blot out love if you blot your signature on a love letter, and will blot out the job if it is a work application you are signing.

X ray: Because you have the vision to see and shape your soul, harm will never come too close. You are the essence of your being. Your attention is focused on the bare bones of a blatantly obvious situation. Being empowered, you will prosper and radiate happiness to those who know you.

Yacht: To be sailing means you have reached serenity. Being in control of your emotions and the course of your life, you will blissfully sail through a summery month or two of calm waters.

Zipper: Zipping up means you are wise to take extra safety precautions. You will be closing a matter with certain finality. Opening a zipper means you will be zipping around on short and speedy missions to put your life in order.

Zodiac: You are connecting with spiritual cycles harmonizing in your soul. You may or may not quite understand what silver or gold magic the stars are weaving for you, but all will become clear on the astral plane. You will be meeting a wealth of new people you will treasure for time immemorial.

Zoo: You wish to unleash your animal instincts and wild parts of yourself you feel empathy for. If you are patient, heaven will reveal your destiny.

[108]

Dream Magic,
nighttime potions,
and magical sleep formulas

Y ou are in control of thoughts that enter your mind and can analyze a nightmare to determine whether it relates to your past or if it is a premonitory vision of a misfortune that you have the power to avert by avoiding the circumstance. ¶ Dream spells work in perfect harmony with dreams. A dream or a chance thought produces an effect on your feelings. But a purposeful thought is the beginning of action that attains a positive result. The oils and herbal teas used in these concoctions are readily available in supermarkets, drug-, and health food stores.

BIRTHDAY WISH DREAM

After the "Happy Birthday" song at your birthday party, collect the candles from your birthday cake and keep one slice of the cake for your spell. At five minutes before the special hour of midnight, light the candles in the reserved slice of your birthday cake while you are alone in front of a mirror. Let the candle flames reflect the thoughts into your mind from the mirror. On the stroke of midnight, blow out the candles. Your birthday dream will reveal how your wish will come true.

VALENTINE'S DAY
SWEETHEART DREAM

On February 14, take a candle that is the color of the moon, either white or silver. Stroke a few drops of lavender oil onto the candle from the candle tip, representing the North Pole, to the center, then up from the candle base's South Pole toward the center. Lavender, ruled by Mercury, enhances mental and physical communication, so concentrate your wishes on the center of the candle. ¶ Light the candle in front of a mirror. On clean white paper write your name above the name of the one you love. Fold the paper so your name and his or hers are face to face. Place the paper under your pillow for romance in your dreams. Speak his or her name and your name once as you look into the mirror and snuff out the candle. The person of your dreams will appear in your sweet dream. ¶ The flame of your love story can also be rekindled later, because you have magnetically and emotionally charged the candle with lavender oil. Simply relight the candle for sweet dreams in the future.

EASTER LOVE, MYSTERY, AND MAGIC

On Good Friday place a sprig of rosemary under your pillow. Ruled by the sun, it will bring sunshine into your dreams and waking hours. When you settle your head on your pillow to sleep, say: *"Tonight I will dream of love."* Close your eyes and go to sleep to dream of romance. ¶ On Easter Saturday say: *"Tonight I will dream of mystery."* The dream will reveal your destiny. ¶ On Easter Sunday light a yellow candle, stare into the flame, and say: *"Tonight, magic will make my Easter wishes come true."* Snuff out the candle, open your bedroom window, and sleep with an open mind. Your wishes will unfold in your dreams and reveal your destiny.¶ The following day, place the rosemary in a handkerchief or a clean white envelope and keep it among your personal possessions. As spring blossoms, your wishes will bloom.

HALLOWEEN DREAMS
TO BE WOOED

Using a ballpoint pen, write the name of the one you desire on the base of a pumpkin. Hollow out the pumpkin to make a pumpkin head featuring eyes, nose, and teeth in the likeness of the object of your affections. Place a lit candle inside and speak your wish: *"Enchanted by passion and by love bewitched, / A romantic glow in (name of person's) heart is fixed. / From this sacred night of All Souls' Eve, / My magic spell is cast to spin and weave."* ¶ As the candle burns, the one you desire will think of you. Snuff the candle out at the moment that you feel is right. Tonight you and he or she will meet in your dreams.

A TWELVE DAYS
OF CHRISTMAS DREAM

At the special hour of midnight on Christmas Eve, light a red candle. Place a dish beside the candle and put a bulb of garlic into it. Immerse the base of the bulb in water. Make a wish and snuff out the candle. Relight the candle every night and replenish the garlic's water supply. On the twelfth night, January 6, sleep with the garlic beside your bed to chase away old demons. New garlic shoots and roots will bless you with a pure New Year you have created. Plant or bury the garlic close to the entrance to your home.

A HAPPY NEW YEAR WISH

On the first new moon of the New Year, when the moon appears as a crescent with its points facing left, take a bay leaf and write your wish in pencil on it. Stand outside facing the moon and kiss the bay leaf three times. Hold the bay leaf on your heart and carry it to your pillow. Place the bay leaf under your pillow, and your dream will reveal how your wish will be fulfilled. In the morning, cast the bay leaf into the breeze from the fingertips of your left hand, the closest hand to your heart.

TO DREAM OF A LOVED ONE
WHO HAS DIED

Light a white candle and in its glow anoint the four corners of your bedroom mirror with Angel Oil potion (seven drops of eucalyptus oil, seven drops of orange oil, and seven drops of rose oil). Place the rest of the potion in a small bowl in front of the candle and say: *"My soul is heaven blessed, / To see (name of person) tonight is my request."* Anoint the center of your forehead, your wrists, and heels with one dab of oil each. Snuff out the candle and dream of one who has passed on but still lives in your heart and soul.

FIVE WAYS
TO DETER NIGHTMARES

Place a stone with a hole through it beside your bed. The nightmare is believed to pass through the hole and dissipate into thin air.¶ Before going to sleep, place a glass or dish of still spring or freshly run tap water beside your bed. Water represents emotions, and pure water will purify disturbance.¶ Collect rainwater to wash your hair in after a full moon. It will neutralize negative thoughts.¶ Place three cloves of garlic beside your bed to absorb negativity. The three cloves represent God, man, and spirit. Garlic, ruled by Mars, will fight for you against evil. In the morning, bury the garlic.¶ Before going to sleep, dwell upon your "champagne moments." These are the successes of your day or previous days, weeks, months, and years. Going to sleep with happy thoughts will attract positive dreams.

TO BANISH A NIGHTMARE

The morning after a nightmare, open your bedroom window and in your bedroom write your nightmare on a clean piece of white paper. Light a new white candle and burn the paper in the candle flame as you say: *"Nightmare burn, / Never return. / No harm will run, / From the nightmare spun."* ¶ Place the paper in a saucer or dish to extinguish it. Cover the ash with one hand and carry the saucer to your bedroom window to cast the ash outside into the wind.

TO REMOVE A NIGHTMARE

When you are ready for bed, make a cup of chamomile tea by infusing a chamomile tea bag or fresh chamomile flowers in a cup of boiling water. Take the brew to your bedroom and light a blue candle in front of your bedroom mirror. Gaze into the flame and concentrate on the circle of light that the flame emits, reflects, and magnifies in your mirror. Drink the chamomile infusion, snuff out the candle, and go to bed. ¶ Lie on your back and imagine that the circle of gold light that was around the candle flame is now encircling your body like a hoop. Say: *"Please place a golden ring of dreams around me."* When you fall asleep you will have sweet dreams, because no harm can come beyond the ring of dreams.

[116]

TO CHASE AWAY
NIGHTMARES

Light a white candle in front of the mirror on your dressing table. Go to the north corner of your bedroom and sprinkle camphor oil onto your fingertips. Dab the north corner of your bedroom with camphor oil while saying: *"North, south, east and west, / I command fright to leave at my behest."* Do the same in the south, east, and west corners. Wash your hands, snuff out the candle, and go to bed to enjoy a sacred night's sleep.

TO RECALL
A SWEET DREAM

On rising, infuse three twigs of rosemary in a cup or glass of boiling water to drink after your morning beverage.

TO OVERCOME LOVER'S
INSOMNIA

You can release yourself from sleepless nights that dissipate your stamina and waste your emotions. To get to the core of your emotions and to the feelings of the one you love, eat lettuce. The moon that rules passion also rules lettuce. Pull the outside green leaves off the lettuce until the head of lettuce is reduced to its heart and stub. The bittersweet taste at the heart and core of a lettuce is lactucarium, a natural sleep-inducing sedative. ¶ When you are ready for bed, place a glass of spring or tap water and the lettuce heart on your dressing table and light a pink candle for love, saying: *"Tonight, under the stars and heaven above, / Reveal to me, (name of person), your true love. / If your love is untrue please take your flight, / And leave me to sleep in peace tonight."* ¶ In the bathroom, light a white or silver candle, as the moon also rules these colors. Switch off any electric light in the bathroom and concoct a potion of Sweet Dream Oil (seven drops of geranium oil, seven drops of marjoram oil, and seven drops of ylang-ylang oil). ¶ To induce fresh spiritual vibrations, sprinkle seven drops of Sweet Dream Oil into running bathwater. Relax in the bath and prepare for bed. ¶ Carefully carry the candle along with the remaining oil to your bedroom and place both on a white cloth in front of your bedroom mirror. In candlelight and facing the mirror, eat the lettuce and drink the water, while thinking peacefully that all you reflect upon will return to you. Brush your teeth, to be ready for a dreamer's kiss or words of departure from the one you love. Sprinkle your pillow with a few remaining drops of Sweet Dream Oil. Snuff out the candle and enjoy a sound and sweet night's sleep, during which your lover will visit in your dreams to reveal interest or disinterest. If he or she does not appear in your dream, put him or her out of your mind for a time.

DECISION DIVINATION BATH

When you need to make a decision but are unsure of making the right choice, the correct answer can appear in a dream whenever you request. ¶ Light a silver, gold, or white candle in your bathroom. With all electric lights out, rub three lavender heads between the palms of your hands and sprinkle the seeds or flowers into running bathwater. (Seven drops of lavender oil can be used instead.) Before getting into the bath, say: *"This water is consecrated and holy, it is heaven blessed."* Soak for a while, dwell upon your query, then dress in clean nightwear for bed. ¶ Carry the candle to your bedroom. On an unused bay leaf, write the question that you wish to be answered during sleep. Place the bay leaf under your pillow and snuff out the candle. Get into bed and say: *"I pray the answer to my dilemma will appear tonight in my dream."* You will dream of the answer. If when you wake you feel the answer has not arrived, it may be that you simply have not recalled your dream. Leave the bay leaf under your pillow. Relight the candle while getting ready for bed on the following night and snuff the candle out before retiring. The answer will be there in your dreams.

LOVE DIVINATION BATH

Buy yourself a glass bottle of colored bubble bath, preferably made from natural rather than synthetic ingredients.¶ Concoct a lover's potion using three sprigs of fresh rosemary, ground with a mortar and pestle or with a rolling pin until you have a mixture of pulp and sprigs, and five drops of lavender oil or five lavender heads.¶ During hours of darkness, light two candles in your bathroom, one representing you, the other your lover. Run a bath, adding twice the amount of bubbles that you would normally use. Agitate the lover's potion and rosemary sprigs into the running bathwater. Place the bottle of bubble bath where you will be able to see into it while you are lying in the bath.¶ Relax in the bath and center your mind on the bubbles' reflections, an alternative to seeing visions in a crystal ball. Shapes and pictures that are premonitions of the future will appear in individual bubbles. Multiple bubbles will also reveal clairvoyant pictures. So too will the bubble bath bottle if you stare into it.¶ A bubble bath bottle is a perfect glass of contemplation, a bath-time alternative to a crystal ball. Light, especially candle-light moving as it shines through, will present pictures of people and objects in the glass and in your mind's eye.

TO INVITE A SPECIAL LOVER
INTO YOUR DREAMS

At midnight, light a golden candle in your bedroom. Write your lover's name on a small piece of white paper and put the piece of paper beside your bed. Place a vase with a rose in it on top of the paper bearing your lover's name. Look into the candle flame and dwell upon your lover, saying: *"Tonight I shall dream of true love."* Snuff out the candle, get into bed, and enjoy loving dreams. When the rose fades, remove the petals and scatter your dreams into the wind.

EARLY-MORNING
WAKE-UP CALL

To make yourself wake up at a certain hour, before going to sleep, bang your head on the pillow the appropriate number of times corresponding to the hour that you would like to wake. For example, bang your head seven times to wake at seven o'clock.

TO FIND A LOST OBJECT
IN A DREAM

Concentrate upon the lost article for a few moments
before sleeping. The article's hiding place is hidden
away in the deep recesses of your subconscious and can
be found in your dream because you have set your mind
on retrieval.

MEMORIZING BY SLEEP

Learning material that will be on an exam before going
to sleep is said to make absorbing information easier
than simply using daytime learning. This method
works for some people but not for all. You must be
determined to wake with the work memorized. A poem
is a good experiment.

TO VISIT A LOVED ONE
WHILE HE OR SHE SLEEPS

Your spirit naturally leaves your body and returns
during sleep. While you are sleeping, you may like to
visit your lover's dreams or see whether he or she is
sleeping alone. ¶ On the night of a full moon, light a
white or silver candle, because the moon rules both
colors. Switch off any electric lighting and stare into the
candle flame for a few minutes, thinking of the person
and the place you would like to visit in your dreams.
On a piece of clean white paper, write the name of the

person and the place you wish to visit during sleep. Snuff out the candle, place the piece of paper under your pillow, and sleep on it.¶ In the morning you should be able to recall having seen your chosen person in your chosen location without being seen by anyone else.

TO SEE A LOVED ONE
WHO HAS DIED

Say a prayer or speak aloud before going to sleep: *"I wish to visit (name of person) tonight in my sleep."* You will meet that person in your dreams. If you wake up thinking a meeting didn't take place, try again the following night. It could be that you didn't recall the reunion. A meeting usually takes place on the night you ask or within a few days or a week. You most certainly will meet, because love is the link.

SLEEP-TALKING TRUTHS

A loved one who trusts your intentions to be good will easily tell you the truth while he or she sleeps. To receive a response, make known your purpose to know the truth, but be loving. Hold the sleeper's hand. Gently, slowly, and clearly repeat: *"You are asleep and will tell me what I wish to know."* The faint whisper of an answer you receive at first will grow louder and stronger, and may surprise you. You must stay calm. Never startle the sleeper by speaking in any way other than softly. Agitated tones will wake and frighten the sleeper.¶ Once the sleeper replies, the channel is open for you to ask the questions you would like to have answered. It may take a few nights of repetition before you receive a response, but if love governs your interaction, your sweet dreamer will reply.

MY WISH IS
YOUR COMMAND

Mesmerism can also encourage a sleeper to adopt your suggestions and carry out your requests. Once a rapport has been established, gently repeat: *"You are under my influence and will do as I ask."* Then quietly say what it is you wish the person to do in waking life, such as giving up smoking, being more confident, or buying you chocolates or flowers on romantic impulse.

[123]

THE ANSWER ON THE WINGS
OF A PRAYER

To sleep on a problem seldom fails to bring nighttime counsel. Before going to sleep, say a prayer or ask aloud for a solution to appear in your dream. You will awaken with the answer, revitalized by sleep. The isolated problem will then miraculously be viewed with enlightened perspective.

Sleep Superstitions

- To sleep with your head toward north and your feet south is said to be healthy and rejuvenating. Powerful electrical currents that run through the earth from the North to the South Pole will recharge you.

- It is believed that an elderly person who sleeps in the same room as a young child will unwittingly sap some of the youngster's vitality.

- You will have a bad night's sleep if you do not continue to make your bed once you begin.

Good Night!

To get out of bed on the
wrong side is said to induce
                                    a bad mood.

    Peonies placed in the
    bedroom are said to deter
                                    nightmares.

*M*ay you always have sweet dreams and may all your sweet dreams come true. May this book make good bedtime reading and be a good friend in dark hours. May it help link your soul to heaven and lay your fears to rest. Like stars twinkling in the night, may all your dreams sparkle with clairvoyant vision so that you always follow your dreams. Dreams really do come true.

[127]

FIRST EDITION

For information on Time Warner Trade Publishing's
online publishing program, visit
www.ipublish.com.

Library of Congress Cataloging-in-Publication Data

Kemp, Gillian.
The dream book : dream spells, nighttime potions and
rituals, and other magical sleep formulas / by Gillian
Kemp — 1st ed.
p. cm.
ISBN 0-316-39972-8
1. Dream interpretation. 2. Magic. I. Title.
BF1091 .K385 2001
154.6'3 — dc21

2001038020

10 9 8 7 6 5 4 3 2 1

Lake Book

Book design by
JULIA SEDYKH DESIGN

Printed in the United States of America